Fantastic Fish

by Lily Schell
Illustrated by Natalya Karpova

BLASTOFF!
MISSIONS

BELLWETHER MEDIA
MINNEAPOLIS, MN

Blastoff! Missions takes you on a learning adventure! Colorful illustrations and exciting narratives highlight cool facts about our world and beyond. Read the mission goals and follow the narrative to gain knowledge, build reading skills, and have fun!

BLASTOFF!
MISSIONS

Traditional Nonfiction

BLASTOFF! READER

BLASTOFF! Beginners

BLASTOFF! DISCOVERY

BLASTOFF! MISSIONS

Narrative Nonfiction

Blastoff! Universe

MISSION GOALS

> FIND YOUR SIGHT WORDS IN THE BOOK.

> IDENTIFY THE TRAITS OF FISH.

> THINK OF QUESTIONS TO ASK WHILE YOU READ.

This edition first published in 2023 by Bellwether Media, Inc.

No part of this publication may be reproduced in whole or in part without written permission of the publisher. For information regarding permission, write to Bellwether Media, Inc., Attention: Permissions Department, 6012 Blue Circle Drive, Minnetonka, MN 55343.

Library of Congress Cataloging-in-Publication Data

Names: Schell, Lily, author.
Title: Fantastic fish / by Lily Schell.
Description: Minneapolis, MN : Bellwether Media, Inc., 2023. | Series: Blastoff! Missions. Amazing animal classes | Includes bibliographical references and index. | Audience: Ages 5-8 | Audience: Grades 2-3 | Summary: "Vibrant illustrations accompany information about fish. The narrative nonfiction text is intended for students in kindergarten through third grade"-- Provided by publisher.
Identifiers: LCCN 2022020226 (print) | LCCN 2022020227 (ebook) | ISBN 9781644876497 (library binding) | ISBN 9781648348334 (paperback) | ISBN 9781648346958 (ebook)
Subjects: LCSH: Fishes--Juvenile literature.
Classification: LCC QL617.2 .S335 2023 (print) | LCC QL617.2 (ebook) | DDC 597--dc23/eng/20220504
LC record available at https://lccn.loc.gov/2022020226
LC ebook record available at https://lccn.loc.gov/2022020227

Text copyright © 2023 by Bellwether Media, Inc. BLASTOFF! MISSIONS and associated logos are trademarks and/or registered trademarks of Bellwether Media, Inc.

Editor: Betsy Rathburn   Designer: Andrea Schneider

Printed in the United States of America, North Mankato, MN.

This is **Blastoff Jimmy**! He is here to help you on your mission and share fun facts along the way!

Table of Contents

An Underwater Tour!

Strap on your **snorkel** for an underwater tour! Today we will explore some of Earth's 34,000 fish **species**.

snorkel

gills

These **cold-blooded** creatures have backbones. They breathe through **gills**. Let's dive in!

Freshwater Fun

scales

Here we are at North America's Lake Superior! Look for the shimmering **scales** of a rainbow trout.

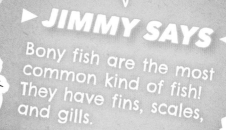

▶ **JIMMY SAYS** ◀

Bony fish are the most common kind of fish! They have fins, scales, and gills.

rainbow trout

These **bony fish** like cool, clear **freshwater**. There go some now!

lamprey

Yikes! This terrifying lamprey is a fish, too.

It is a **jawless fish**. They are one of the oldest kinds of fish!

red-bellied
piranhas

Watch for danger as we travel to South America's Amazon River. Those red-bellied piranhas have sharp teeth!

JIMMY SAYS
Unlike most fish, electric eels must come to the surface to breathe.

electric eel

Keep your feet off the bottom, too. Electric eels give off painful shocks!

Coral Reef Creatures

coral reef

parrotfish

clownfish

Our next stop is a colorful **coral reef**. Thousands of fish live here!

Over here, an eel lies in wait.
See the parrotfish and clownfish
fleeing from it? Even the puffer fish
puffed up to stay safe!

puffer fish

eel

Let's get a closer look at these pygmy sea horses. They do not look like other fish. But they each still have fins, a backbone, and a gill!

pygmy sea horse

fin

15

Off to the Open Ocean

There are plenty of fish here in the open ocean. That hammerhead shark swimming past is a fish.

hammerhead shark

manta ray

▶ **JIMMY SAYS** ◀

Sharks and rays have bendy skeletons. They are made of a material called cartilage.

This manta ray above us is one, too!

Deep Sea Dangers

Wow! It is dark this deep in the ocean. But these lanternfish light our way.

Stay away from that far light, though. An anglerfish waits with big teeth!

lanternfish

anglerfish

It is time to come up for air. But there are so many more fish in the sea!

Look for more fantastic fish next time you dive below the surface!

Fish Facts

have
backbones

have gills

live underwater

21

Glossary

bony fish–fish that have skeletons made of bone; bony fish, jawless fish, and cartilaginous fish are the three main kinds of fish.

cold-blooded–having a body temperature that changes with the outside temperature

coral reef–a structure made of coral that usually grows in shallow seawater

freshwater–water that is not salty

gills–body parts that help fish breathe

jawless fish–fish that do not have jaws; jawless fish, bony fish, and cartilaginous fish are the three main kinds of fish.

scales–hard plates that cover the bodies of some fish

snorkel–a tube that people can breathe through while underwater

species–kinds of animals

To Learn More

AT THE LIBRARY

Kurtz, Kevin. *Fish for Kids: A Junior Scientist's Guide to Diverse Habitats, Colorful Species, and Life Underwater.* Emeryville, Calif.: Rockridge Press, 2021.

Sabelko, Rebecca. *Ocean Animals.* Minneapolis, Minn.: Bellwether Media, 2023.

Shumaker, Debra Kempf. *Freaky, Funky Fish: Odd Facts about Fascinating Fish.* Philadelphia, Pa.: RP Kids, 2021.

ON THE WEB

FACTSURFER

Factsurfer.com gives you a safe, fun way to find more information.

1. Go to www.factsurfer.com.

2. Enter "fantastic fish" into the search box and click 🔍.

3. Select your book cover to see a list of related content.

BEYOND THE MISSION

> WHICH FISH FROM THE BOOK WAS YOUR FAVORITE? WHY?

> DRAW A PICTURE OF A NEW KIND OF FISH. WHAT IS ITS NAME?

> DO YOU THINK IT WOULD BE EASY TO HAVE A PET FISH? WHY OR WHY NOT?

Index